Robert Williams Buchanan, John Cramb

Jerusalem in 1860

A series of photographic views taken expressly for this work

Robert Williams Buchanan, John Cramb

Jerusalem in 1860
A series of photographic views taken expressly for this work

ISBN/EAN: 9783741184376

Manufactured in Europe, USA, Canada, Australia, Japa

Cover: Foto ©Thomas Meinert / pixelio.de

Manufactured and distributed by brebook publishing software
(www.brebook.com)

Robert Williams Buchanan, John Cramb

Jerusalem in 1860

JERUSALEM IN 1860:

A

SERIES OF PHOTOGRAPHIC VIEWS,

TAKEN EXPRESSLY FOR THIS WORK

BY

JOHN CRAMB, PHOTOGRAPHER TO THE QUEEN.

WITH DESCRIPTIVE LETTERPRESS

BY THE

REV. ROBERT BUCHANAN, D.D.,

AUTHOR OF "A CLERICAL FURLOUGH," ETC.

GLASGOW:
WILLIAM COLLINS, BUCHANAN STREET.
MDCCCLX.

PREFACE.

PECULIAR fascination belongs to the Holy Land. The fact that it was the cradle of the Christian faith, and the scene of nearly all the great events which the Bible records, must ever invest it with an undying interest to every Christian mind. Hence the ever-increasing demand for information regarding it. To meet this demand travellers of late years have done a great deal by the pen, and artists have done not a little by the pencil. Hitherto, however, not much use has been made, in illustrating the sacred scenes of Palestine, of the marvellous modern art of Photography. And yet it cannot be doubted that there is, perhaps, no other country in the world upon the illustration of which it is more important, that the extraordinary powers of this beautiful art should be brought to bear. What those who cannot themselves visit the Holy Land desire, above all things, to have, is something which they can rely upon as an exact and faithful representation of it. A merely fine picture is not, in this case, what they care to possess, but a life-likeness of the original. This *desideratum* Photography alone can, with absolute certainty, supply. To realize it is the design of the present work. The localities which it exhibits are among the most notable in Judea, and they are so arranged as to form a continuous and connected series. The Letterpress Descriptions, with which the Views are accompanied, will be found not merely to throw light on the Views themselves, but on the geographical features, topographical associations, and Scripture history of the various scenes which they represent.

JERUSALEM FROM THE ROAD TO BETHANY N'

JERUSALEM FROM ROAD TO BETHANY.

—

PECULIAR interest attaches to the spot from the immediate neighbourhood of which this view was taken. It was here that Jesus shed tears over the coming ruin of the city. This affecting and impressive incident occurred, as Scripture relates, on the occasion of His approaching Jerusalem from Bethany, not many days before his crucifixion; and when the attending crowds were shouting, "Blessed be the king that cometh in the name of the Lord." In approaching Jerusalem from Bethany, the city is entirely hidden from view by the intervening Mount of Olives, till the last ridge of the hill is turned. The road reaches this ridge at a point where the hill sinks down considerably, forming a kind of hollow or pass between the Mount of Offence on the left, and the much higher summit of Olivet itself, on the right. On rounding this lower ridge, the city bursts all at once, and for the first time, upon the view. The Valley of Jehoshaphat, which here narrows into a deep rocky ravine, all but precipitous on both sides, is immediately in front. Beyond it, and close at hand, is the Haram, with its lofty wall, enclosing the sacred ground upon which stood the ancient Temple, and now occupied by the magnificent Mosque of Omar. Behind the Haram the city itself spreads out, and in the direction of Zion rises high above it. It was this very scene, such as it existed at the period above alluded to, the sudden opening of which upon the eyes of our Lord called forth the pathetic lamentation which the evangelist records: "And when He was come near, He beheld the city, and wept over it, saying, If thou hadst known, even thou, at least in this thy day, the things which belong unto thy peace! but now they are hid from thine eyes," (Luke xix. 41, 42). Although there is no tradition regarding the locality of this particular event, it needs nothing but a careful comparison of the place, with the terms of the Scripture narrative, to enable any one who visits the spot to satisfy himself that nowhere else but here could the incident have occurred.

The road from Bethany, to which reference has been made, passes close to the right hand of the foreground of the picture; the stony foreground itself occupies, as will be seen, the very brink of the deep defile of the Valley of Jehoshaphat, which crosses the picture from right to left, but is here quite hidden, by its depth and narrowness, from the spectator's sight. The upper part of the steep bank which forms the farther side of the valley, rises up beyond it, surmounted by the wall of the Haram, which, at the point where it turns off at right-angles from the valley, is seventy feet in height. The plateau occupied by the Haram—the ancient enclosure of the Temple—is the Moriah of Scripture. The continuation of the ridge to the left of the Haram is Ophel, which terminates in an abrupt rocky descent at a little distance beyond the extreme left of the picture, and near to the Pool of Siloam. Beyond Ophel it will be observed that there is a hollow, from which the ground again rises towards Zion, which appears in the distance on the left. The hollow is part of the Valley of the Tyropœon, which, in Scripture times, separated Moriah from Zion; and the course of which can be still distinctly traced, though it has been to a large extent filled up by the debris of the city, and by the immense accumulations of the rubbish which, in the course of ages, has been thrown into it. The building with a dome upon one end of it, which stands in the left angle of the Haram, is the Mosque of El Achsa. It was originally a Christian church.

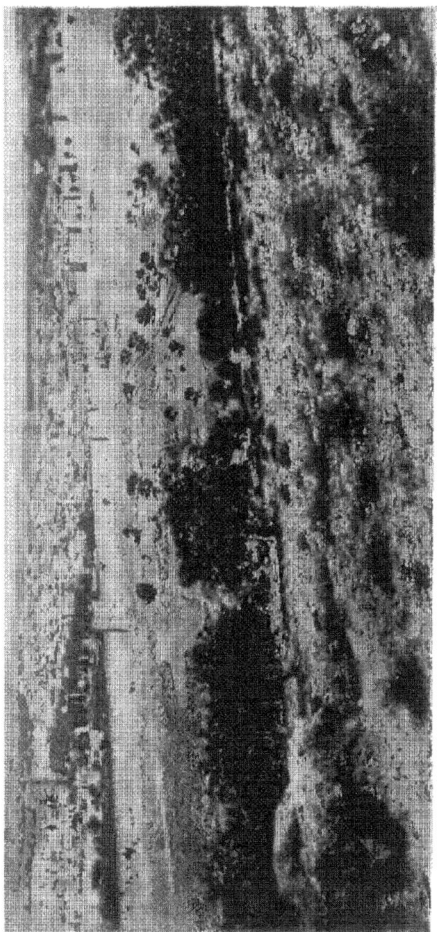

JERUSALEM FROM THE ROAD TO BETHANY Nº 2

JERUSALEM FROM ROAD TO BETHANY.

(SECOND VIEW.)

THE present view is taken from nearly the same point as the preceding one, and forms a continuation of it. Instead of looking, as in the former case, across the valley westwards, the spectator is here looking up the valley northwards. In the background is the rugged slope of Olivet, thickly strewn, towards the valley at its base, with the trees from which it takes its distinctive name. The road from Bethany slants downwards from the left, across the picture, but hidden by the trees and by the rapid fall of the hill. It reaches the bottom of the valley beyond, and below the dense mass of wood on the right. Ascending from that point, it may be seen, as it rises above the trees and winds up the opposite side of the valley, towards St. Stephen's gate, where it enters the city. That gate, though partially concealed by a projecting angle of the city wall, will be noticed a little to the right of the centre of the picture. The city wall itself, though Saracenic, and only about 300 years old, is built, to a large extent, on this side of the city, on the boundaries of the ancient wall. The lower courses of the masonry, and especially along the side of the Haram, are in many places, manifestly, altogether different from those above, and of a much older date. Not only are the stones of immensely greater size,—many of them being from twenty-five to thirty feet in length, and of corresponding thickness,—but they are bevelled round the edges in a style known to be that of Hebrew times. The Haram terminates northwards at a point a little to the left of St. Stephen's gate. Beyond this point the wall is of lower elevation, and the larger stones disappear, as will be distinctly seen by a close inspection of the present view. The dark line of buildings, in deep shadow, running inwards from the point of the wall now indicated, form the northern boundary of the Haram. The part of the city lying beyond that line, and to the right of it, corresponds to the ancient Bezethar, the outermost and lowest section of the city in Scripture times. Immediately to the left of it, and beyond the Temple area, was Akra, the second or middle division of the city. Still farther to the left, and on the highest ground of all, was Zion, the stronghold of the ancient Jerusalem, but which is not included in the present view. Right over the northern and north-western parts of the city, appears a finely wooded and comparatively level expanse, stretching onwards to the base of the hill of Scopus, and still covered all over with the ruins and foundations of numerous buildings. Far away beyond these woods, in the extreme distance, a range of hills bounds the view. The loftiest peak of these hills, showing itself like a sharp point on the sky-line of the picture, is Neby Samwil, so called from a tradition that upon that commanding height the Prophet Samuel was buried. Recent and careful investigations have led to the conclusion that it is the ancient Mizpeh of Saul. It overtops the whole of the elevated hill country around it; and this circumstance undoubtedly favours the supposition of its being the Scripture Mizpeh,—a name which signifies a watchtower. It is in the midst of the territory of Saul's tribe, which was that of Benjamin; and standing upon it, he could survey the entire country, from the Mediterranean on the west, to the mountains of Ammon and Moab, on the farther side of the Jordan valley, on the east. A finer position, therefore, for a watchtower could not well be conceived.

JERUSALEM FROM THE NORTH

JERUSALEM FROM THE NORTH-WEST.

THE four preceding views have exhibited the chief objects of interest along the eastern side of the city, and also those which occupy its central parts, between the St. Stephen's and Damascus gates. The present view places the spectator once more outside of the city; but this time on the opposite side from that of the Mount of Olives. He is here standing on the north-western face of the city, and not far from the Damascus gate, which is seen to the left of the centre of the city wall, half-hidden by the mounds which swell up in front of it. The foreground, as will be noticed, is under cultivation; as is, indeed, the greater part of the extended plateau on this side of the city. The ground is literally covered with small stones; but these, in the climate of Syria, are not without their use in the fields, as they serve to protect the soil from the heat of the sun, and thereby cause it to retain its moisture much longer than it could do otherwise.

Between the wall and the mounds by which the lower part of it is concealed, there is a deep and pretty broad hollow, immediately beneath it, and which runs along the whole of this side of Jerusalem. It is evidently, to a large extent, artificial, and seems to have been dug to strengthen the defences of the place. Along this trench-like hollow, about a hundred yards beyond the extreme left of the picture, is the entrance to those remarkable excavations which have been recently discovered, and which penetrate a great way under the city. The entrance is very narrow, and, even at the distance of a few yards, is entirely hidden by weeds and rubbish. It has been formed simply by the loosening of a few stones at the basement of the wall, where it rests on the solid rock. Within, it expands immediately into a large cavern, beyond which it stretches on in a long and intricate succession of similar chambers and galleries, all evidently artificial; and still bearing, in every direction, distinct traces of the tools by which they have been cut. They are manifestly old quarries, from which, in all probability, the materials for many of the chief buildings of the ancient city were dug. They have been explored to the distance of one-third of a mile from the entrance, but it is probable that a more thorough examination might show their extent to be much greater.

The large building in the distance, on the extreme right, is the Latin Convent of St. Salvador. It belonged originally to the Georgians, but was bought and enlarged by the Latins in 1561, when they were driven out of their convent on Zion. It contains about fifty monks, one-half of whom are Italians, and the other half Spaniards. It is the chief convent of the Latin or Roman Church in Syria. The Greek Church has eight convents and five nunneries in the city. The Armenians have also several religious houses, and their great convent on Mount Zion is both the largest and richest in Jerusalem. The smaller sects—viz., the Syrians, Copts, and Abyssinians—have also conventual establishments, though of a less considerable kind. The numbers connected with the different Christian churches in the Holy City is said, according to a late enumeration, to be as follows:—Greeks, 1,500; Latins, 1,200; Armenians, 280; Syrians, Copts, and Abyssinians, 150; Greek Catholics, 110; and Protestants, 100.

The large solid square tower on the sky-line in the centre of the picture is that of Hippicus, to which another opportunity of referring will occur. A little beyond it, but out of sight, is the Jaffa gate, towards which the wall runs from the Latin Convent in a direction a little to the east of south.

To the left of Hippicus appear the domes of the Church of the Holy Sepulchre, already described. The large white modern building, in the middle distance on the extreme left, is the back part of the Austrian Hospice, of which a partial front view appeared in the picture of the Via Dolorosa.

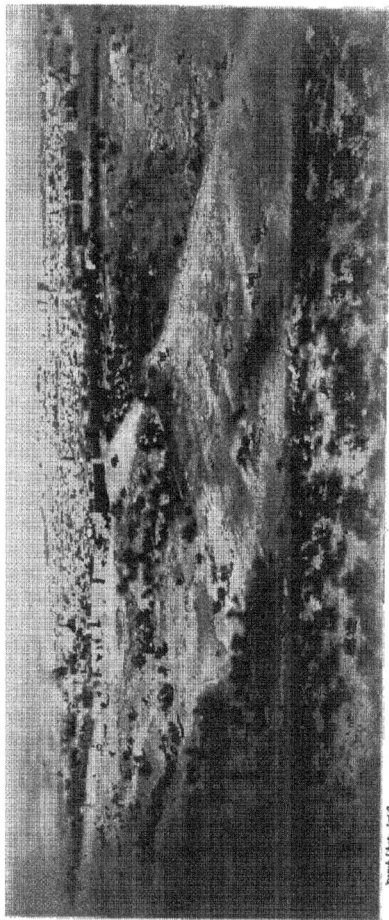

JERUSALEM FROM THE NORTH-EAST

JERUSALEM FROM SCOPUS.

＊

BEFORE presenting the city in detail, we shall conduct the spectator to the most favourable position for obtaining a comprehensive view of the whole. For this purpose we must ask him to ascend northwards out of the Valley of Gihon, and crossing the open ground which stretches along the west and north-west sides of Jerusalem, to take his stand upon the Hill of Scopus. This hill is due north from the city, and about a mile distant from it. It was here that Titus, the Roman general, pitched his camp on the occasion of the terrible siege in which the city was destroyed. It commands, as the picture shows, a complete view, not only of the city itself, but of the country all around it. Scopus itself is a continuation of Olivet, which fronts the eastern side of Jerusalem, and overhangs the deep valley of Jehoshaphat, along the margin of which that side of the city runs. At the point where the range to which Olivet belongs, comes opposite to the northern extremity of the city, it bends gradually round to the west, and thus enfolds the city on its northern side also. It is from the brow of this part of the hill—called Scopus, on account of the extensive prospect which it affords—that our view is taken. In the foreground is the finely wooded slope, by which the hill itself descends into the valley below. The valley, it will be observed, begins here to recede farther and farther away from the present city wall; but there is abundant evidence to show that the entire space included between the present northern and north-western wall on the one side, and the upper part of the valley on the other, was, in the time of our Lord, covered by the gardens and suburban residences of the wealthier citizens. It is quite certain, indeed, from the statements of Josephus, and from other sources of evidence, that this extensive suburb was actually enclosed by the wall built by Agrippa, about twelve years after the crucifixion. Only on this side, indeed, was it possible to enlarge the city, hemmed in as it was on every other quarter by the deep valleys on the brink of which it stands. The extent to which nature has thus entrenched Jerusalem may be seen at a glance, by looking at this view of the city, from Scopus, in the light of the following statement. The angle of the wall which occupies the centre of the picture, marks the north-eastern extremity, both of the ancient and of the modern city. Following the wall from this angle towards the left, it has the Valley of Jehoshaphat immediately beneath. Down this valley ran the brook Kedron, though now it flows only during a few days of the rainiest season of the year. About a fourth of a mile beyond the point where this eastern wall terminates, at the extreme left of the picture, it meets the Valley of Hinnom, which sweeps round the south side of the city, under the lofty and rocky heights of Zion. In the direction Zion appears, right over the angle of the wall already noticed, and at the opposite extremity of the city. Rounding the south side of the city the Valley of Hinnom—opening out, as it ascends, into the Valley of Gihon—takes a north-westerly course; and keeps close under the city wall till it advances to a point a little beyond the Tower of Hippicus, whose square and massive form will be easily recognized in the picture, to the right of the highest part of Zion, and about half-way between it and the Latin convent,—the large white building which stands at the most distant part of the city on the extreme right. Only, therefore, between the Tower of Hippicus and the north-eastern angle of the city wall is there any level ground adjacent to the city. Immediately within the eastern wall of the city, and near the middle of it, appears the Mosque of Omar, with its majestic dome, covering the sacred site of the ancient Temple of Jerusalem. In subsequent views the principal buildings, and most interesting portions of the city, will be seen on a larger scale; but their relative position will be better understood by a careful study of the city as a whole, and as presented in the present picture.

POOL OF BETHESDA & CHURCH OF ST ANNE

POOL OF BETHESDA AND CHURCH OF ST. ANNE.

WE have now passed from the exterior to the interior of the city; and the view here presented is taken from the eastern wall, at a point a little to the north of St. Stephen's gate. The spectator is supposed to be standing near the left corner of the foreground, and is looking diagonally across the city, in a south-westerly direction, towards Mount Zion, which occupies the distance on the right. The foreground, it will be noticed, is a scene of complete desolation,—nothing appears but the foundations of the buildings of a former age. The same aspect belongs, indeed, to the greater part of the space, enclosed within the walls, of the northern section of the modern city. It will be observed that a high wall stretches out from the left side of the picture towards the centre; above which there springs up a lofty and beautiful minaret. This wall has a very deep hollow at its base, marked in the picture by the deep shadow that hangs over it, and to which tradition has assigned the name of the Pool of Bethesda. Though this hollow, or trench, is now dry, it bears unequivocal marks of having, in former times, been filled with water. The wall in question rests on the solid rock, which has evidently been cut down to a great depth in the same perpendicular with the wall itself, for the purpose of forming this excavation. The huge fosse thus laboriously dug, probably served the purpose both of a public reservoir, and at the same time of a defensive moat to protect the Castle of Antonia, which occupied the space immediately beyond the wall. It is 360 feet in length, 130 feet in breadth, and 75 feet in depth. The depth originally was, no doubt, much greater, as the rubbish of centuries has been shot into it. Its length also would appear to have been considerably more extended than now, for at the west end it has been arched over, and modern houses now stand above what, anciently, must have been a continuation of this gigantic moat. The sides of it still bear the traces of having been thick-coated with cement, so as to prevent any leakage of the water with which it appears to have been filled. Speaking on the subject of this remarkable work, the celebrated American traveller, Dr. Robinson, says, "I hold it probable that this excavation was anciently carried quite through the ridge of Bezetha, along the northern side of Antonia to the north-west corner, thus forming the deep trench which (Josephus informs us) separated the fortress from the neighbouring hill." He supposes that the Romans, in making their approaches in the great siege to the Castle of Antonia, and to the Temple which it defended, filled up the western part of the trench so as to facilitate their hostile operations; thus reducing its extent, and leaving it to exhibit, in connection with the influence of the many other changes the city has undergone, the appearance it now assumes. There is nothing whatever to sanction the tradition which identifies it with Bethesda, which would seem, from the Scripture narrative, to have been a pool of a much smaller and shallower kind.

Near the foreground of the picture, toward the right, are the remains of the ancient Church of St. Anne; founded originally in honour of the mother of the Virgin Mary, and standing on the site where, according to monkish tradition, the mother of Jesus was born. During the period of the Crusades there was attached to it a Convent of Benedictine Nuns; which, when Jerusalem fell finally into the hands of the Saracens, was converted into a Muslem College. It is now the property of the French Emperor, to whom it was lately made over by the Sultan.

The other prominent buildings which appear in the remoter parts of the picture will be described in connection with those subsequent views in which they are presented in greater detail.

MOUNT OF OLIVES & VALLEY OF JEHOSAPHAT

MOUNT OF OLIVES AND VALLEY OF JEHOSHAPHAT.

◆

HIS view is taken from nearly the same point as the preceding one. The spectator is still stand-ing upon Scopus; but instead of looking southward, as before, across the Holy City, in the direction of Zion, he is here looking south-east, towards the Mount of Olives. It is that sacred height, crowned with the mosque and minaret which occupy the site of the ancient Church of the Ascension, which the present photograph chiefly represents. The Mount of Olives rises, as will be seen from the picture, high above the city, its elevation exceeding that of even the loftiest point of Zion by about 200 feet. Its entire height from the bed of the valley of Jehoshaphat, at its base, is fully 500 feet. Across this hill lay the wind-ing mountain path by which the Saviour was wont, at the close of the day, to retire from Jerusalem to Bethany,—the town of Lazarus, and of his sisters, Mary and Martha,—which lay on its opposite or eastern side. There is no reason to doubt that the path of the present day is the same which existed in Scripture times, and it may without difficulty be traced in the picture, nearly all the way from the city gate to the crest of the hill. The only gate on the eastern side of the city is that of St. Stephen, so named from a tradition, that by it the proto-martyr of the Christian Church was led forth to be stoned to death. This gate is hard by the northern side of the great area which formed the sacred enclosure of the ancient Temple, and where, during His visits to Jerusalem, so much of the Saviour's time was spent. By this gate, therefore, both from its proximity to the Temple, and from its being the natural egress in going towards Bethany, Jesus, on the occasions in question, was no doubt accustomed to issue from the city. The gate of Stephen is exactly at the point where the wall reaches the extreme right of the picture. From that point a slanting path is distinctly visible, descending obliquely to the bottom of the valley. The little walled enclosure, having numerous olive trees within and around it, lying a very little to the left of the bed of the valley, and to which the path spoken of leads on, is the traditional Gethsemane. This tradition, indeed, like many others connected with the Scripture scenes around and within the Holy City, is by no means universally received. Gethsemane was evidently resorted to by Jesus as a place of seclusion and retirement; and such a character could hardly belong to a place both so close to the city, and so near to a public thoroughfare. The road from Jericho to Jerusalem, the chief approach to the Holy City from the east, passes it on one side, and the much frequented mountain path from Bethany passes it on the other. Some sequestered spot farther up the valley—and the view now presented evidently shows that the sloping sides and hollows around the base of Olivet must have offered many such quiet retreats—would appear to correspond much better to the requirements of the Scripture narrative, than the one which tradition has chosen. But to return to the path from Jerusalem to Bethany: From the corner of the wall of the traditional Gethsemane, this path may be seen running nearly straight up the hill to its very top, at right angles to the terrace-like strata of the limestone rock which appear cropping out, one above another, along the face of the hill.

The Church of the Ascension, already alluded to, was built by the Empress Helena, mother of the Roman Emperor Constantine, on the spot where the mosque and minaret now stand. The site of the Church was chosen in deference to a tradition, that from this precise spot on the summit of the mount the Saviour ascended up to heaven. Scripture expressly relates that He led out His disciples "as far as to Bethany," and that there, "while He blessed them, He was parted from them, and carried up into heaven," (Luke xxiv. 50, 51). With that explicit statement, the tradition in question cannot properly be reconciled.

In the centre of the picture, and immediately beyond the Mount of Olives, appears the Mount of Offence, where Solomon erected altars to the false gods of the heathen. The remote distance beyond is the hill country lying between Jerusalem and Bethlehem.

POOL OF HEZEKIAH FROM THE CITADEL

POOL OF HEZEKIAH.

T is a singular historical fact, that though standing on the summit level of a mountain country, and in so comparatively dry and warm a climate as that of Palestine, Jerusalem never seems to have experienced, even in its longest sieges, any want of water. There are no rivers or streams near it; for "the brook Kedron," even in ancient times, in all probability flowed only during the rains. Of natural fountains, or wells, there are also very few, with the exception of the small Fountain of the Virgin, near the lower end of the Valley of Jehoshaphat, the Pool of Siloam, beneath the extremity of Ophel, and the well of En Rogel, some hundred yards beyond Siloam, down the Valley of the Kedron. There are no others in the neighbourhood of the city. For the supply of so immense a population as that of ancient Jerusalem, these scanty sources must have proved altogether inadequate. But this deficiency was amply provided for by that elaborate and extensive system of cisterns, of which the remains are still to be seen anywhere throughout the city. One of the most remarkable of these is the pool which occupies the foreground of the present picture. The view of it, which is here exhibited, is taken from the top of the Tower of Hippicus, which is high enough to enable the spectator to see quite into the pool, enclosed though it be, all round, within a dense cluster of buildings; and, at the same time, to include in the same prospect the whole city and country northwards to Scopus.

This pool is called the Pool of Hezekiah, on account of its answering so exactly to a work of this kind, which Scripture mentions as having been executed by that pious and patriotic king. It is told of him, as one of his memorable acts, that "he made a pool and a conduit, and brought water into the city," (2 Kings, xx. 20); and as indicating the locality of this pool, and the source from whence it was fed, it is further stated, that "he stopped the upper watercourse of Gihon, and brought it straight down to the west side of the city of David," (2 Chron. xxxii. 30). The upper watercourse of Gihon, if not stopped, would naturally flow down that valley towards Hinnom and the lower Valley of the Kedron. Instead of leaving it to take this direction, which would have carried it past the *south* side of the City of David, he led it along the higher level, by a conduit, to the *west* side of the city. The relative positions of this pool and the upper watercourse of Gihon, correspond to this description. The Pool of Hezekiah itself is 240 feet long, by 144 feet wide. Its original extent was, however, evidently much greater, as recent excavations prove that it reached at least sixty feet farther north than the point where it at present terminates. The bottom of the pool is formed by the natural rock, which bears the marks of having been artificially levelled and covered with cement.

Besides this larger class of cisterns, of which the vast subterranean tank beneath the Haram, already noticed, is another remarkable example, almost every house of any note had its own private cistern. These smaller cisterns are usually hewn out of the solid rock, and are generally vaulted chambers, into which the water, during the rains, was conducted from the courts and roofs of the houses. In the house occupied by the Prussian Consul, there are no fewer than four of these cisterns, one of which is thirty feet square, by twenty feet deep. It was by these means that the city enjoyed that abundant supply of water, which, even during the protracted siege by Titus, and when so enormous a population was crowded within the walls, seems never to have failed. Though thousands perished from hunger, no hint occurs in the history of that fatal siege by Josephus, that their sufferings were ever aggravated by thirst. Nor is it unworthy of notice, in connection with this interesting fact, that the hostile armies by which Jerusalem was at different times assailed, were compelled, more than once, to raise the siege of the city, from the entire want of water in the country around.

The buildings to the left of the Pool of Hezekiah, and immediately beyond it, are the French Hospital and the Coptic Convent. In the centre of the picture there is an excellent view of the Church of the Holy Sepulchre. In this view the smaller dome, which, in the large picture of the same church, appeared right over the massive campanile, is seen in its proper position, as rising above the central part of the nave. A small part, of what remains of the façade of the church, appears in deep shadow, close to the campanile on the right.

CHURCH OF THE HOLY SEPULCHRE.

— ◆ —

THE statements of Scripture with regard to the place of our Lord's crucifixion and burial, are much too general to determine its precise locality. It was "without the gate," (Heb. xiii. 12), though still "nigh to the city," (John xix. 20). It was beside a burying-place—for its name was Golgotha, the place of a skull; and in its vicinity there was a garden. Beyond these particulars nothing is told; and obviously they are such as might apply to many more places than one. The flight of the Christians to Pella before the great siege, in which the city perished—their long absence from it—the changes which the desolations of war produced, both upon the city itself and upon the whole country round—render it in the highest degree improbable that any certain knowledge, as to the spot where the Lord lay, should have been handed down. During the first three centuries history is absolutely silent upon the subject; and after the lapse of so long a time, in such an age, and after such social and political convulsions as had meanwhile intervened, it is not likely that what was so completely forgotten should have again become known.

The story upon the strength of which a different conclusion was long unhesitatingly accepted, is too palpably incredible, to satisfy the inquisitorial and searching strictness of modern inquiry. That the Empress Helena visited Jerusalem in the early part of the fourth century, and that under her auspices there took place, what is significantly known as "the invention of the cross," is no doubt true; but that the real cross, the real Golgotha, and the real sepulchre, were, as that story tells, actually discovered, it would require a very blind credulity to believe. The tale is too obviously fabulous to need serious confutation. Over the site where the alleged discovery was made, and which must have been far *within* the limits of the ancient, as it is of the modern city, a church was first built between the years 326 and 335. This church was destroyed by the Persians when they took the city in 614. It was rebuilt a few years after, but was again destroyed in 1010 by the Khalif Hâkim. Subsequently to the conquest of Jerusalem by the Crusaders, in 1099, it was once more restored and enlarged; and it is chiefly the church of that date that remains to the present day. It was, indeed, extensively injured, and many parts of it destroyed by fire, so recently as the year 1808; but with the exception of the domes, the greater part of the building, such as it is seen in the picture, belongs to the era of the Crusades. The large ragged-looking dome towards the left, with its flying buttresses resting on the adjacent buildings connected with it, overhangs the alleged Holy Sepulchre. This rotunda is sixty-seven feet in diameter, and in the centre of its floor stands the little marble structure, cased outside with common stone, and within which is the so-called tomb of our Lord. Towards the northern side of the rotunda is the alleged spot where He appeared on the morning of His resurrection to Mary Magdalene; and a little farther on, and within the transept, is the place where He is said to have first shown himself to His virgin mother. The square tower, with buttresses at the angles, and with a smaller dome, seen over it, is the remains of the massive campanile, once five storeys in height, which projects from the façade of the church, to the left of the entrance. Beyond this tower, and extending away to the right, is the nave of the building— now the Greek Church—with the many dependent chapels and crypts that are ranged around it. The place of "the invention (finding) of the cross" is at the eastern extremity of the building, i. e., at the opposite end from the rotunda. The rotunda, as not being the exclusive property of any one of the rival churches, but open to them all, is in shameful disrepair. The nave, which forms the Greek Church, is in better order, though its decorations are much more gaudy than graceful. Among the many startling sights that are shown within this remarkable building, are the tomb of Melchizedec, and the tomb of Adam! But the most shameful spectacle of all that is exhibited in this ostensibly sacred place, is the coarse and impious imposture of the holy fire, which is annually kindled within the sepulchre, to the joy and admiration of the half-frantic pilgrims, with whom, at these times, the rotunda is densely thronged. This fire, lighted by the presiding ecclesiastic within the sepulchre, and then thrust through a hole in the side of it, that the superstitious pilgrims may light their candles at it, is pretended to be kindled by the immediate descent of fire from heaven! It is a relief to the truly devout mind to think that the place where these shameful scenes are enacted, is certainly *not* the sepulchre of our Lord.

TOWER OF DAVID & ANGLICAN CHURCH

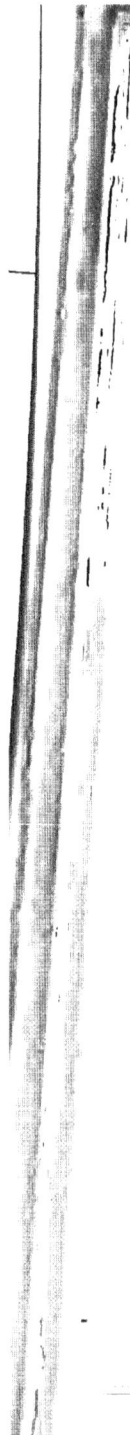

TOWER OF HIPPICUS AND ANGLICAN CHURCH.

— ✦ — ‥

THE Tower of Hippicus was built by Herod the Great, and was so called in memory of a friend who had fallen in battle. Josephus describes it with great minuteness. It stood at the north-western angle of Zion, upon a rocky crest, which gave it a commanding position. It was built of enormous bevelled stones, and to the height of thirty cubits was one solid mass. Above this solid part of the tower there were chambers for the guards, and the whole was crowned with battlements. When Titus destroyed the city he preserved, Josephus informs us, this particular tower, and two others near it. Its own rock-like solidity, however, had probably something to do in saving it from the general ruin; and when Adrian rebuilt and fortified Jerusalem, fifty years thereafter, advantage was no doubt taken of this relic of the ancient strengths of the city in erecting the new citadel. It still stood in the time of the Crusades, and was known among them by the name of the Castle or Tower of David. When the Mohammedans, in the thirteenth century, overthrew the walls of the city, this tower was left standing. Such a chain of historical evidence, certifying the fact of its having been actually preserved, coupled with its known aspect and character, have furnished ample materials for conclusively identifying it with the nearer and larger of the two structures which occupy the centre of this picture. The tower thus presented answers exactly to the account of Josephus as regards the great size of the stones, the peculiar style of the masonry, and the fact of its being solid throughout. The view of it here given is taken from an open space inside of the city wall, and a little to the north of the Jaffa gate. The point of view is sufficiently elevated to carry the eye of the spectator over the city wall to the right, and to trace its course from the angle which the Jaffa gate occupies, onwards along the brow of Zion. The dark height in the distance, on the extreme right, is the summit of the Hill of Evil Counsel, rising beyond the narrow Valley of Hinnom, which lies deep down between that hill and Zion.

The great interest which attaches to the Tower of Hippicus is not derived exclusively from its historical associations, and its high antiquity. It has an interest of quite a distinct and different kind, as throwing a flood of light on the topography of the ancient city. Josephus expressly mentions it as the point from the immediate vicinity of which the three walls of the city took their start,—viz, the first wall, or that of Zion, the original city of David; the second wall, which swept round Akra, the next and later section of the city; and the third wall, or that of Bezetha, the suburban and lowest part of the city, and the latest built of all. Having such a fixed point as Hippicus from which to begin in tracing these walls, the nature of the ground, the remains of them that still exist, and the historical allusions of Scripture history, and of Josephus, have gone far to settle, with at least a great approximation to certainty, their actual course.

Immediately to the left of the Tower of Hippicus appears in the distance the Anglican Church, attached to which is the house till lately occupied by the British Consul. It is a commodious place of worship, erected since the founding of the Jerusalem bishopric, and capable of containing from two to three hundred worshippers. The court beside it, and around which are the houses of the clergy, is hidden by the Tower of Hippicus. There is no other Protestant church in the city.

The dome upon the sky-line near to the left of the picture is that of a large Jewish Synagogue, recently built on Mount Zion, but of which a nearer and more perfect view will afterwards be presented. The spectator, in this view, is looking a little to the east of south; and as in that direction the ground begins to fall a very short way behind the Anglican Church, the greater part of Zion is altogether out of sight.

VIA DOLOROSA

VIA DOLOROSA.

LTHOUGH the traditions that cluster around this celebrated street are, perhaps, without a single exception, utterly destitute of foundation, and are, many of them, altogether childish, it is nevertheless impossible not to view it with peculiar interest. It owes its name to the assumption of its being the identical and mournful route, along which our Lord was led from Pilate's judgment-hall, to the place of execution at Calvary. And though there is no evidence to justify this conclusion, and much to contradict it, the fact that it has been so long received with implicit faith by the crowds of pilgrims who annually throng to Jerusalem from the Greek, Latin, and Armenian churches, and the place which its various scenes and stories occupy in Italian art, can hardly fail, as a recent traveller observes, to make every thoughtful traveller regard it with at least a passing emotion. The view of it which is here presented was taken from the roof of Max's private hotel. The spectator is looking eastwards, and the Mount of Olives is in the distance, with the mosque and minaret which occupy the site of the Church of the Ascension, on the sky-line, about mid-way between the centre and the right. On the extreme left, within a wall, is the handsome new Austrian Hospice and conventual establishment, built within the last three years. The tall and handsome minaret, in the centre of the picture, belongs to the mosque attached to the Serai, or Governor's house, near the north-west angle of the Haram. Near that spot, but extending much beyond it, stood, as explained in connection with a previous view, the palace and fortress of Antonia, where was Pilate's judgment-hall, and his ordinary official residence as the Roman governor. The Via Dolorosa, beginning at that point, advances westwards into the city. It is seen, in the picture, as it comes forward from the distance, passing under an arch, and running along outside the wall of the Austrian Hospice, till, turning off sharply to the right, near the foreground of the picture, it disappears among the houses. It leads on finally, and still farther to the right,—though its continuation is not embraced in this view,—to the Church of the Holy Sepulchre. Wherever Calvary may have been situated, it certainly was not at the place assigned to it by monkish tradition. Our Lord was crucified "without the gate," and it has been conclusively proved that the traditional Calvary must have been quite within, probably far *within* the city of Pilate's time. The probability is that the mournful procession, whose course tradition professes so minutely to trace along this *Via Dolorosa*, never entered it at all, but rather passed out at once from the city by the gate of Stephen, close by the Castle of Antonia, into the open country, outside the walls.

In the wall at the Governor's house, where this street begins, are two arches built up. Here stood, it is said, the *Santa Scala*, or Sacred Stair, which led up to Pilate's judgment-hall. This is the stair which pilgrims now painfully climb upon their knees in the Church of St. John Lateran at Rome! A little farther on is the Church of the Flagellation, where it is said Jesus was scourged. Beyond this a short way is the arch seen in the picture, and where Pilate, according to the tradition, brought forth the bleeding Saviour, when he presented him to the Jews, and said, "Behold the man!" As the traveller pursues his course along this famous street, he has pointed out to him in succession, as he proceeds from the *Ecce Homo* arch to the Church of Calvary, and of the Holy Sepulchre, the house of Dives, with the stone in front of it on which Lazarus sat—the house on which Jesus leaned when bending under the weight of his cross, and on which his shoulder made an impression which still remains—the house of Veronica, who presented the Saviour with the handkerchief with which he wiped his bleeding brows, and which is still exhibited to the faithful, on certain great occasions, in St. Peter's at Rome,—though Lucca and Turin also claim to have, each of them, the true relic thus superstitiously venerated. To mention these things is enough to expose their worse than puerility. None of them were ever heard of earlier than the fourteenth century. They are among the things which serve not to consecrate, but to desecrate the Holy City.

MOSQUE OF OMAR

THE HARAM AND MOSQUE OF OMAR.

THIS fine view of the interior of the Haram is taken from the roof of the Governor's house, and the spectator is looking a little to the east of south. The Haram-esh-Sherif, or Noble Sanctuary, is upwards of 1500 feet in length from north to south, and considerably exceeds 900 feet in breadth. Josephus describes the area of the Temple enclosure as forming a square; and on the supposition of its not having extended farther north than about 150 feet beyond the great Mosque, its form might, with perfect propriety, be so described. Those who have most carefully examined the question are satisfied that the Temple enclosure did terminate at the point now mentioned. Its boundaries on the other three sides—the east, south, and west—are such as to identify themselves. The nature of the ground, and the character of the substructions by which the enclosure is faced up on these sides, leave no room to doubt that they represent the exact limits of the ancient Temple area. This area was not originally level. In King David's time it was the rugged, uneven top of Mount Moriah, in the midst of which was the threshing-floor of Araunah the Jebusite. Being selected as the site for the great national Temple of God's ancient people, it was afterwards levelled artificially, and also extended, especially to the south, east, and west, upon arched work, faced up and supported externally by massive substruction walls. The lower parts at least of these retaining walls, with their massive masonry, as also the arches underneath, still remain. It has also been ascertained, on good historical and other evidence, that the great Mosque stands upon the exact site of the Hebrew Temple. This splendid Mosque, commonly called by the Muslems the Kubbet-es-Sukkrah, or Dome of the Rock, owes this peculiar name to the fact, that immediately under the dome there is a large mass of rock, rough and unhewn, rising about five feet above the floor, and about sixty feet in diameter. When the Temple of Solomon was built this rock is supposed to have been preserved in memory of its having been the divinely chosen spot, occupied originally by Araunah's threshing-floor, and that afterwards the great altar of burnt-offering was erected over it. There is abundant historical proof to show that this rock was so regarded by the Jews in the early centuries of the Christian era. Fifty years after the destruction of the city and temple by Titus, the Emperor Adrian built on this site a temple to Jupiter, and placed an equestrian statue of himself on the spot, which was known to have been occupied by the Holy of Holies in the time of the Jews. This statue existed in the days of Jerome, in the fourth century, and the exact position, therefore, occupied by the Temple cannot be matter of dispute. The Mosque which now covers that sacred site is said to have been founded by the Khalif Omar, towards the close of the seventh century. It is an octagon, each of the eight sides of which is 67 feet in length. The central part of the edifice, crowned with its noble dome, is 148 feet in diameter. The dome itself is covered with lead. The windows which light the interior are filled with stained glass of exquisite brilliancy, and the piers between the windows are overlaid with glazed tiles of bright colours, and formed into elaborate arabesque patterns.

The small elegant building, to the left of the great Mosque, is the Kubbet-es-Silsilah, or Dome of the Chain, built, some say, as a model of the great Dome of the Rock. The fine Mosque of El-Aksa appears in the distance, to the right, built originally as a Christian church, by the Emperor Justinian, in the sixth century. It occupies the south-western angle of the Haram. It is 272 feet long, and 184 wide. It has evidently undergone many alterations. Its columns and piers are partly Roman and partly Saracenic. Besides the various gates which led into the Temple area of old, upon its own level, recent discoveries have shown that it had an underground approach from the south, which, ascending through a long colonnade or crypt, emerged into the court above. The great fountain beneath the Temple court has also been lately explored. It is 50 feet in depth, and about 750 feet in circumference, and into it the water from the Pools of Solomon seems to have been conveyed.

The open space in the foreground of the picture, as well as the site covered by the modern Governor's house, was occupied anciently by the great palace and fortress of Antonia, built originally by the Maccabees. It was afterwards the official residence of the Roman Governors of Judea, and here, there can be little doubt, it was that our Saviour was judged and condemned.

THE JEWS' QUARTER AND NEW SYNAGOGUE.

THIS view is taken from a point within the city wall, and near to the Zion gate. That gate is on the south side of the city, and on the very summit of Zion. Outside of it, Zion stretches on for about one-third of a mile, till it reaches the precipitous descent into the Valley of Hinnom. In this line between Zion gate and the southern extremity of Zion, there is a small Armenian convent, which, according to one of two rival traditions, occupies the site of the house of Caiaphas, and where the spot is pointed out where Peter denied his Lord. Farther on, and nearer the brow of the hill, are the buildings which are said to cover the tomb of David, and the tombs of the kings. The whole of the space thus alluded to, is beyond the wall of the modern city; and this large portion of Zion, extending northwards to the Jaffa gate and the Valley of Gihon, and southwards to Ophel and the Pool of Siloam, is still, at the present day, literally "ploughed as a field."

Within the wall, as the view now exhibited sufficiently shows, the aspect of this crowning part of the ancient Jerusalem is ruinous and desolate in the extreme. The foreground is little else than a mass of rubbish. In the remoter part of the picture, the upper part of the Jews' Quarter appears. The little domes on the house-tops form one of the characteristic features of the modern city. When seen in the moonlight, they give it the look of a huge oriental burying-place; and truly it is little else than a city of the dead. Beyond the farthest point embraced in the picture, the hill of Zion slopes rapidly down towards the hollow between it and the Haram,—that is, towards the Valley of the Tyropœon. That eastern face of Zion belongs, in great part, to the Jews' Quarter, so that it is only the upper portion of it which is seen in the present view.

There are four cities in the Holy Land which the Jews hold sacred: Hebron in the south; Safed, the "city set on an hill," among the mountains of Galilee, in the north; Tiberias on the shores of the well-known lake; and Jerusalem. In each of these cities there is a considerable body of resident Jews; but by much the largest number is found in Jerusalem, whose very dust they love and reverence. It is difficult to ascertain their numbers accurately; but in the four cities above-mentioned there are certainly not fewer than 10,000 of the Hebrew race. The number in Jerusalem alone is said to amount to about 6,000. They are chiefly from the various countries of Europe—the majority from Germany, Poland, and the Lower Danube. The greater part of them are very poor, and are subsisted chiefly by the alms of their brethren in other lands. They have ten or twelve synagogues in Jerusalem, but most of these are very small. Within the last two or three years, however, they have built a new and much finer synagogue than any which they previously possessed. Its large and lofty dome, towering high above all the other buildings around it, forms a conspicuous object in the present view. In connection with the property they have recently acquired, and the establishments they have erected in the neighbourhood of the city, this more imposing religious edifice would seem to indicate that their prospects are improving in the land of their fathers. In such a place as Jerusalem, where trade and commerce can hardly be said to exist, and where industry of every kind is repressed by an unintelligent and oppressive government, there is, indeed, but little scope for social progress. The times, however, are significant of approaching change in many places, and not least in the land of Israel.

www.ingramcontent.com/pod-product-compliance
Lightning Source LLC
Chambersburg PA
CBHW021527270326
41930CB00008B/1137

* 9 7 8 3 7 4 1 1 8 4 3 7 6 *